FAIRIES

Other Books by Freddie Langeler

Children of the Stars

Children of the Earth

For information, write to Kabouter Products,
1241 21st Street, Oakland, CA 94607. USA

Text: Annemarie Dragt and Dagmar Traub
ISBN 1-56937-104-0
Library of Congress Catalog Number:#95-83183

Printed in Hong Kong

FAIRIES

By

Freddie Langeler

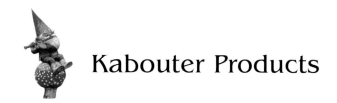

Kabouter Products

Elves, fairies, and friends at their afternoon tea
Eat wild strawberry cake with sesame.
Sweet acorn delight, mushroom cheese on the side.
Drinking raindrop sky nectar, sprites are satisfied.

To the sound of the reed pipe they dance and sing,
Enjoying the day, fairies leap and swing.
"Let's share our pleasure and write everyone:
Invite them to celebrate midsummer's sun."

"We can tell secret tales and put on our wings.
We'll jump over redwoods and count oak tree rings.
This ancient forest, our home and our care
We'll share as we feast and guard all that is rare."

Fairies and gnomes, and a circle of elves
Invite all they can think of besides themselves
Who treasure Nature. They write eagerly:
Their letters a bond to the friends who will be.

Susie YoungScribe has just learned to write.
Little Greenbee helps her spelling look right.
Elves lick honey-glue corners, add the beeswax seal
Each finished letter gives a satisfied feel.

The elves have formed one long working line;
It runs like clockwork, with a group of nine;
Bring the ink, write and think, check once more;
Lick the flap, stamp a seal—and out the door!

Fairy Air Mail Service in action:
"Send your letters with us—get satisfaction!"
Fairies in hurry come racing along—
"Please take our letters to where they belong!"

Edward Elf ascends up into the sky
Teaching the little elves how to fly.
"Spread out your arms and open your heart
Feel the air, greet the sky, ready to start."

"Think happy thoughts!" is the recipe.
"Decide what to think and you will be free."
Secret magic for flying like a fairy:
"Be light as a feather, and never weary."

Barry Beetle, most reliable courier,
Is always polite and can persevere.
Pursue, persist, follow up and remind,
All his mail is on time; he is never behind.

Tucked under his wing the first R.S.V.P,
From Adam Acorn, sprite of the old oak tree.
"My present is blueberry-acorn pie;
Eat just one bite and you'll float in the sky."

One invitation goes up in the trees.
Here Simon Squirrel stores nuts and helps bees.
He hears many tales of the earth long ago
From old giant redwoods who stand in a row.

Wendy Wings and Bernina Butterfly
Sit together high up in the sky.
With letter in hand Wendy flew round the world,
Fastest of fairies, wings completely unfurled.

"Bernina, please come to celebrate
With all kinds of creatures, one hundred and eight.
Please bring your secret ability
That helps caterpillars grow wings and be free."

"I'm delighted to come. I'll bring a rainbow
To color the wings with a special glow.
Right now, let's enjoy what helps me to soar:
Some buttercup tea, sipped each day at four."

Eager elf chefs chop and cook day and night,
Preparing the feast with care, and delight.
Young elves run errands and cart baskets of fruit.
Older ones stir and taste: add more horseradish root!

Alvin Elfling looks on in his checkered hat,
He sees nature's bounty mixed into a vat
Of fresh fairy sky nectar, a special brew
Which helps one to taste and know what is true.

Hazelnut squash steams over the fire.
Seasoned with magic, it lets you acquire
The skill to speak and understand
The tongues of all animals and all lands.

While everyone's busy, the smallest elves find
A great hamper of food in the pantry behind
The kitchen. Much desiring this treasure chest,
They gather up sweets and hide all the rest.

They think no one sees as they flit out the door
To the secret green hillside to eat still more.
Joy and fear show on faces that take up the dare.
"Little ones: listen! It's better to share."

"Those who take all good things for themselves
Become duller, more heavy than regular elves.
With bellies so full they can't win fairy sprints,
And can't hear winds whisper; their hearts become flints."

Midsummer guests gather in the golden lea,
One group settles under a huge redwood tree.
Edward Elf, Susie YoungScribe, and various friends,
Sit and savor their tea and all nature lends.

Simon Squirrel tells his story: "Long long ago,
When the meadows were covered with mistletoe,
Human children would dream-travel to our realm,
And learn from the guardians of redwood and elm."

"Wearing our wings endowed with great speed,
Children flew over tree tops, and planted new seeds.
Graceful-eared elves deep of hearing did sing
And all creatures felt as one, part of every thing."

"When they woke from their dreams so long ago,
The children remembered. What they did know
Is now only whispered. Elves, gnomes, and birds—
Let's find the dream children and pass on these words!"

At their secret place elves feel guilty and sad.
Having drunk the truth nectar they now must add
Sore hearts to full bellies. This moment they know
This sort of pleasure ends soon and brings woe.

"Come with me, elflings," urges Milton the Mole.
He saw them sneak-eating from his home, a snug hole.
Just about to climb out and leave for the feast,
Knowing their state, his furry brow creased.

"Ed Junior, Polly Prickle!—I know you feel sad.
Heavy thoughts ruin your flying. That's very bad.
You'll do much better if you help for a while.
Come find a lost treasure: the hidden Dream Child."

Under a mushroom a child lies asleep.
A mouse serves as pillow; they're both dreaming deep.
"Hurrah! We have found it!" elves happily shout,
They rejoice and dance and jump about.

The child is dreaming of being a fairy
With longish ears and a smile quite merry.
Drawn to the midsummer fest and its power
The dream child can dance, fly for many an hour.

Ed Junior and Polly Prickle now feel light,
They thank Milton Mole for this special sight.
More and more dreamchildren will come again.
The forest will teach them. Now magic won't end.

Freddie Langeler was a well-known Dutch illustrator in the 1920's. From 1913 on, Freddie Langeler worked regularly for Uitgeverij Kluitman in the Netherlands. She illustrated many children's books, some of which became classics and are enjoyed by children up to the present day. This is the first time that Langeler's work is published in the United States.